Norman Rockwell's AMERICAN HOLIDAYS

Written by Milton Garrison

CRESCENT BOOKS
New York

Contents

Merry-Go-Round (1947)

8

Introduction

For six decades, starting in 1913, Norman Rockwell celebrated America's red letter days with an abundance of works. He, like the century, was in his teens. Until his death, Norman Rockwell continued recording the American experience faithfully and in faultless detail. He started painting in this country's horse-and-buggy days and continued into the space age.

Through those generations, Norman Rockwell shared and reflected his fellow Americans' interests, sorrows, and joys. From the beginning, the holidays were an occasion for joy, and he recorded those joys with empathy, drama, humor, and accuracy. The sympathy and fidelity with which Norman Rockwell portrayed the human experience accounts for the lasting regard and affection we have for his paintings.

Another factor is present in this universal popularity: Norman Rockwell's works evoke a remembrance of times past. In our memory, as in his paintings, life was simpler, relationships more straightforward. Families celebrated the holidays together, they were closer knit. Many Americans of today are too young to have experienced that time of innocence, of high hopes and common purpose, of country lanes and wood smoke, of children playing safely on clean city streets.

That is the America we find in Norman Rockwell's paintings. It is a comfortable place, and even if we were never there, we enjoy visiting it.

John Sargeant and Chief Konkapot (1972-1976)

10

Chapter 1

Our National Holidays

Norman Rockwell recalled that as a small boy he sketched Admiral George Dewey's flagship, USS Olympia, as it steamed into New York Harbor at the close of the Spanish-American War, in 1898. He continued to depict our national holidays, when the air and the water were clean, when it was inconceivable that an American president could tell a lie and when we assumed good intentions in one another. We knew our neighbors better then; it made it easier for us to like one another. Norman Rockwell's oblique approach to his subjects and his humor are evident throughout his work displayed here.

DO UNTO OTHERS
AS YOU WOULD HAVE THEM
DO UNTO YOU

Golden Rule (1961)

Martin Luther King's Birthday

On January 20, 1986, the United States celebrated the birthday of the great civil rights leader and humanitarian Martin Luther King Jr. for the first time. This national honor to a black American was a long time coming. Although Martin Luther King Jr. was born on January 15, the national holiday celebrating his birth is now held on the third Monday in January.

Martin Luther King's birthday is a national holiday that celebrates the life and accomplishments of a unique leader. He preached both non-violence and the adamant pursuit of racial equality in an era marked by riots, unrest, murder and violence against black and white advocates of civil rights.

Norman Rockwell's paintings on the civil rights struggle during the 1960s reveal a great deal about the artist's sharp insight and unfailing decency.

The paintings make no frontal attack on the violence, the cruelty, or the sheer injustice of institutionalized bigotry. But they illustrate sharply the human consequences of bigotry and the violence it produces.

It seems the artist, like so many Americans of his time, longed for an end to racism and violence, a return to fair play and decency for all Americans. It also seems obvious that Martin Luther King Jr. personified the best hope for these goals.

Dr. King's Career

Born in 1929, in Atlanta, Georgia, Martin Luther King Jr. was the son of a Baptist minister. He received a bachelor of divinity degree himself, and a bachelor of arts degree from Morehouse College.

Boston University conferred a doctorate on him in 1954, one year after he had risen to national prominence in Alabama. From that time forward, he was a leader in the national civil rights movement. Always advocating peaceful means and non-violence, he helped forge the Southern Christian Leadership Conference and coordinated the Freedom Rides and sit-ins that battled institutionalized segregation in that era.

The Problem We All Live With (1964)

16

Southern Justice (1965)

Martin Luther King's Dream

In the summer of 1963, Dr. King helped organize the March on Washington. As many as a million people assembled in the nation's capital for a peaceful demonstration for civil rights. His speech that day, facing the Mall before the brooding statue of the seated Lincoln, proclaimed for all America the essence of the civil rights movement and its goals. The eloquence of his "I have a dream" speech continues to touch and inspire us.

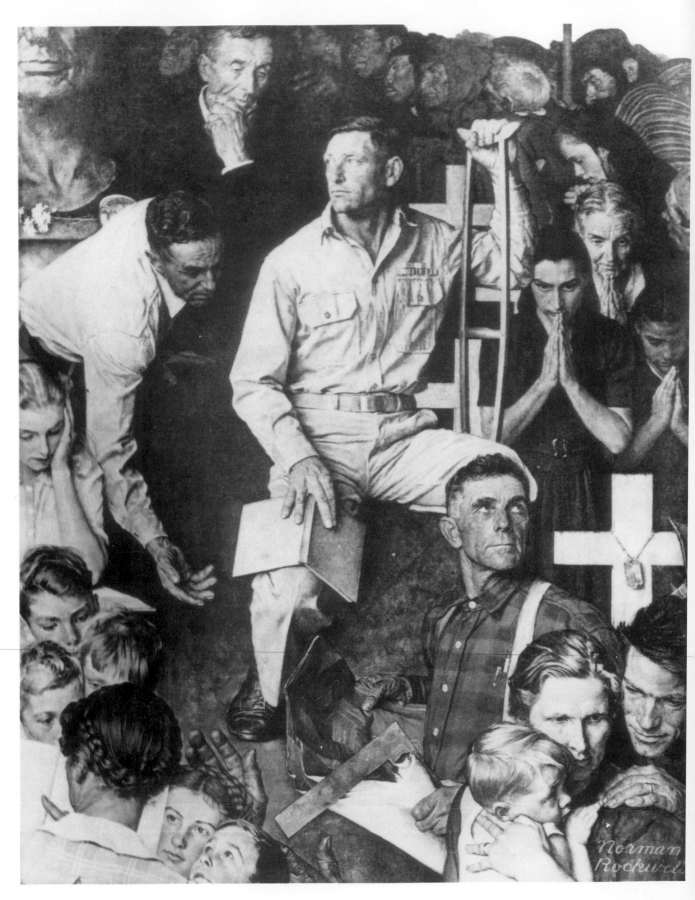

18 *The Long Shadow of Lincoln (1945)*

Presidents Day

Presidents Day, the third Monday in February, is a modern innovation. By an Act of Congress, we now honor all the presidents, even the ones nobody can quite place. To be sure, Lincoln's birthday is still the occasion for partisan gatherings by the political party he founded, and the Democrats memorialize Thomas Jefferson (born March 12) and Andrew Jackson (born March 15) in the same partisan spirit with Jefferson-Jackson Day celebrations.

It was very different in Norman Rockwell's time. We had fewer heroes then and we made less fuss over them. The exceptions were Washington and Lincoln, each considered peerless in his own way.

The New Tavern Sign (1936)

George Washington's Birthday

George Washington was altogether a more august and daunting figure than Lincoln. For one thing, there was that business with the cherry tree. It was exemplary of the boy Lincoln to brave the snows for a book to read by a flickering fire. But for little George to invite a spanking, admit he'd chopped down the cherry tree with his little hatchet—that was honesty that most flesh-and-blood American children had difficulty relating to. Further, there was that announcement, "Father, I cannot tell a lie." Frailer mortals might try very hard not to tell a lie, but for most kids it was not an impossibility, particularly if the lie in question was a very small "white lie." George Washington, as described in their story-books, was a little daunting.

He had the same effect on adults. There is no recorded instance of Washington cracking a joke, indulging in horseplay or enjoying himself. He had apparently led an upright life.

The source for the cherry-tree fable was Mason Locke Weems, an itinerant book salesman and revival preacher. He wrote a "Life" of Washington in 1806 that had great circulation, if dubious accuracy. It included the cherry-tree story and an account of a conversation with an Indian warrior who shot Washington 17 times with no visible effect.

Our First President

Washington was born into the landed gentry in Virginia, and remained a gentleman farmer all his life. He distinguished himself as a soldier for the British in the French and Indian Wars. Then he returned, as he always did when not serving his country, to the life of a country squire. He joined fellow Virginia aristocrats like Thomas Jefferson and James Madison in resisting royal outrages. So high did his fellow colonists regard his character and his military abilities that he was named commander-in-chief of the Continental Army while still serving as President of the Continental Congress that produced the Declaration of Independence. It appears that he neither sought nor campaigned for this or any other office or distinction.

He led his bedraggled, starving army through repeated defeats to a final and unlikely victory in 1781. Having seen the job through, he resigned his commission and returned to Mount Vernon. In 1787, when the weak Confederation was floundering, he accepted the presidency of the Constitutional Convention. In 1789, he was elected the first American President. He was reelected in 1792 and refused a third term, setting a precedent that was not broken until Franklin D. Roosevelt ran for his third term in 1940. In his farewell address, Washington warned the nation against "entangling foreign alliances." This was the basis for U.S. foreign policy for more than a century.

The New Tavern Sign (1936) 23

24

Abe Lincoln in Illinois (1939)

Abraham Lincoln's Birthday

Lincoln was born February 12, 1809—less than a century before Norman Rockwell—and was slain in 1865. The artist grew up among people who had known Honest Abe as a contemporary, who had read his speeches in the daily papers, and had voted for him or against him.

Lincoln, the Common Man

Lincoln was, among other things, a rail splitter. In an America that was still largely rural, split-rail fences were part of every landscape; and many men, or their fathers, knew the labor and the techniques Lincoln had used to construct them. He had been born in a log cabin. So had many of Norman Rockwell's contemporaries, and many people still lived in them.

His life was a dramatic story, and it reinforces cherished ideas: honesty is the best policy; any American child can grow up to be President. Through it all runs a general affection for Lincoln—Honest Abe, the Rail Splitter, Father Abraham, Old Abe. Americans sensed that he liked them, and they liked him.

Abraham Lincoln Delivering the Gettysburg Address (1942) 27

Lincoln, the President

Lincoln was a man of the people, but he now belongs to the ages. He fascinated Americans, not only because they could relate to his humble origins but because he had achieved greatness. Many authors published book after book, article after article about Lincoln, and the public never seemed to get enough. In all the books, the man that emerged was wise and compassionate. He retained the laconic style and shrewd wit of his frontier breeding, never succumbed to the trappings and pretensions of high office. He was unimpressed with ambassadors and generals. He held the nation together through a cruel and divisive war by the strength of his character. In the darkest days, he acted on his own sense of right and wrong, popular or not, and followed his own wisdom.

As the nation's favorite, Lincoln was a godsend to teachers and parents bent on instilling in children the old-fashioned virtues and values: honesty, industry, modesty.

Lincoln for the Defense (1962)   29

Veterans of Two Wars (1918)

Memorial Day

Memorial Day is also known as Decoration Day. Its first observance was spontaneous and gracious. Early in the Civil War, Southern women went to the fields of recent battles to decorate the graves of both Union and Confederate dead.

Remembering

General John B. Murray, in 1866, proclaimed May 5 as Memorial Day for the Union dead. The Grand Army of the Republic embraced the holiday and made it a national one.

In succeeding generations, men from all the states died in overseas wars, and the nation forgot the bitterness of the Civil War. Quite soon, Southern states observed the national Memorial Day as well as the Confederate Memorial Day.

Death of the G.A.R. (1939)

34

Man Painting Flagpole (1928)

Flag Day

Norman Rockwell captured a younger America's quiet, matter-of-fact devotion to the flag. We had been taking the flag for granted for well over a century when President Woodrow Wilson proclaimed June 14 as Flag Day. Apart from the addition of new stars, the Stars and Stripes has remained our standard since it was adopted by the Continental Congress on June 14, 1777. That flag, the original Old Glory, replaced the Grand Union flag, adopted in 1775, which had the same red and white stripes, but the Union Jack in place of the field of stars.

Betsy Ross

There is no reason to disbelieve the legend that Betsy Ross made the first flag of stars and stripes. Mrs. Ross was a fine seamstress and upholsterer who had sewn "ships colours" for the Pennsylvania State Navy. The Continental Congress, the story goes, sent Robert Morris, George Ross, and George Washington as a Commission to secure a flag. When the Commissioners showed concern about getting the new flag right, Mrs. Ross quickly snipped out a batch of five-pointed stars for them.

Mending the Flag (1922) 37

The Star-Spangled Banner

The comfortable, easy-going affection and respect in which earlier generations of Americans held Old Glory began with children in school, pledging allegiance to the flag. The pledge did not contain the words "under God" until sometime after World War II. In the Boy Scouts and Girl Scouts, children learned the code and procedure for raising, lowering, and displaying the flag; that flying it upside down was a distress signal; that no other flag could be flown or displayed above it, or in a position of greater prominence. Most Americans knew the prescribed way to fold and store the flag. We were taught that a tattered or soiled flag must be respectfully destroyed. Ironically, the only proper way to destroy the flag was to burn it.

Under the Flag (1917)

Saluting the Flag (1917)

40

Independence Day

The Fourth of July appears to have triumphed over the centuries of change and the advances of technology and skepticism. We celebrate it today with the same exuberance that is described in early nineteenth century accounts, and with the same spirit Norman Rockwell portrayed.

The Peals of Liberty

It must have afforded the artist much pleasure to incorporate the Liberty Bell in his paintings. The Liberty Bell was associated in American recollection with Philadelphia and by extension with the Saturday Evening Post, founded there as its masthead proclaimed, "A.D. 1728 by Benj. Franklin." And Norman Rockwell was associated with the Saturday Evening Post. He had painted covers and story illustrations for the magazine from 1916 through 1963. It is part of our folklore that the bell cracked as it rang out the news of the Declaration on July 4, 1776.

Liberty Bell (1976) 43

The Glorious Fourth

Apart from advances in fireworks technology, things have been pretty much the same every Fourth of July since 1776. For most of Norman Rockwell's lifetime, Independence Day parades, like firework displays, were notable more for amateur enthusiasm than for polish, and his paintings reflect this. Tootling bands, out-of-step marchers, and the dangerous tendency of little boys to set off firecrackers, cherry-bombs, and torpedoes were the hallmarks of the old-fashioned Fourth.

Nowadays, in the final decade of the twentieth century, it seems the Fourth of July is the one day when we shrug off suspicion and skepticism and return to the time when Americans believed the best of one another. We cut loose with the same enthusiasm, the same oratory and parades. We are all patriots on the Fourth.

And why not? The day we celebrate is a milestone for mankind. On July 4, 1776, the Continental Congress adopted the Declaration of Independence, which held that all men are created equal and proclaimed the right to life, liberty, and the pursuit of happiness.

SESQUI·CENTENNIAL·CELEBRATION
OF·THE·SIGNING·OF·THE
DECLARATION·OF·INDEPENDENCE

Ben Franklin's Sesquicentennial (1926)   45

Two Plumbers (1951)

Labor Day

Labor Day, the first Monday in September, is a uniquely American holiday, and it has changed considerably as our times have changed. Beginning with the Eighties, it lost some of the drama and tension it previously expressed, when union labor and its political allies flexed their muscles. But Labor Day is well established as a national holiday. It is observed by all Americans. It still marks the end of summer vacations, the sure sign that it is time to prepare for school again, and the occasion for family outings of all sorts.

Labor Awakens

It was very different in Norman Rockwell's time, and especially in the strife-torn years of organizing, strikes, and struggles of the 1920s, 1930s, and 1940s. In those decades, union men and women carried banners and flags in marches.

Apparently, the American labor movement showed no interest in the European idea of celebrating Labor Day on May 1. The shift to the first Monday in September took place in 1882. That first Labor Day parade by 10,000 unionists was around Union Square—named, of course, for the federal union preserved in the recent war.

Most Americans, then as now, were only marginally involved in the labor part of Labor Day. But in a most important sense, they were participants nonetheless. In the earlier years of this century, Labor Day, like the Fourth of July, May Day and Memorial Day, was a time for family outings, picnics, potato-sack races, horseshoes, and pick-up games of softball and baseball.

In a way, the present, relaxed Labor Day honors workingmen and workingwomen in a general way that would probably have pleased Thomas Jefferson and other early Americans who visualized a nation of peaceful and industrious yeoman farmers and mechanics.

Mine America's Coal (1943)   49

50

Disabled Veteran (1944)

Veterans Day

The fourth Monday of October, was designated in 1954 as the day Americans honor the men and women who served in this country's wars.

It incorporates many aspects of Armistice Day, November 11, on which the nation—together with the British, the French, and all the World War I allies—marked the close of the most horrible war men could then imagine.

A Tribute

On Veterans Day we pay tribute to the men and women who have fought in America's wars, a holiday that honors all who served. Armistice Day was a tribute to those who had fallen in battle—and more: a day of renewed dedication and idealism.

It had been called an age of innocence, when we believed that the Unknown Soldier had given his life in the war to end wars, to make the world, in Woodrow Wilson's phrase, "safe for democracy." But more than naiveté was involved. The lesson the First World War taught Americans was the futility of war. At the eleventh hour of the eleventh day of the eleventh month, the nation observed a minute of silence. Then the bands struck up the old tunes—"Pack Up Your Troubles in Your Old Kit Bag," "Tipperary," "Over There"—and the soldiers marched in somber parade.

You Can Trust Me Dad (1917)

The War to End All Wars

It was on November 11, 1918, at 11 a.m., that the Germans applied to the Allies for the armistice that ended the First World War. It had begun in August, 1914, and had slaughtered a generation of young Britons, Germans, and Frenchmen. The United States entered the war on April 16, 1917, and its fresh masses of troops, coupled with American manufacturing capacity, had turned the tide for the exhausted Allies.

The horrors of the Civil War were more than fifty years past; the old people didn't dwell on them. Relatively few men fought in the Spanish-American War, a brief one that had won America a Pacific empire, and no one recalled the toll disease had taken of our soldiers.

Carrying On (1920) 55

World War II

By the time of the Second World War, Norman Rockwell was older. He had shared America's experiences with the harsh realities of the age, and he knew—among other things—that war was no fun. The old cheerful spirit remains in his World War II paintings, but it is tempered by a realistic approach. The underlying mood is one of serious purpose rather than jaunty tours by ambassadors of good will. The nation knows now that its soldiers suffer, are wounded, and die in war. Battle is portrayed as deadly business.

Still, there were happy interludes. Norman Rockwell's stock-character soldier, Willie Gillis, goes through a series of adventures in the peacetime draft army and through much of the war. It was frustrating for Norman Rockwell when the model for Willie, a neighbor boy, shipped out after joining the Navy.

Willie Gillis: Food Package (1941)   57

Homecoming

At last, the war was over, and the men and women came home. The artist welcomed them, paid tribute to their sacrifices, but seldom painted of war again.

But Armistice Day remains the inspiration for a treasured American holiday. In 1921, to honor the dead in the same fashion as our allies who suffered such great losses, the United States sent an American soldier to France. The soldier selected one of the coffins of unidentified American soldiers and an American warship brought the body home for a state burial in Arlington National Cemetery. Ever since, private soldiers of the U.S. Army have done sentry duty at the tomb.

Homecoming Marine (1945)

In Memory

Since 1921, on each Armistice Day and Veterans Day, the President makes the pilgrimage to Arlington Cemetery for a simple, touching tribute. The bugler sounds taps, a squad of riflemen fires three volleys, and the nation honors its war dead.

The remains of unidentified men killed in the Second World War and in Korea have since been interred in the Tomb of the Unknown Soldier, now called the Tomb of the Unknowns.

Willie Gillis in Church (1942)

Something to Be Thankful for (1922)

Chapter II

Special Holidays

In the centuries that stretch back to pre-history, holiday customs have been adopted, adapted, combined, and confused. Pagan celebrations of fertility, of the planting and harvest seasons, of that glimmer in the darkest time of year that made it evident that the days were getting longer again—all these have been incorporated willy-nilly into our special holidays.

Happy New Year (1945)

The New Year

Americans celebrate the new year with the rest of the world. We did not originate the New Year's Eve party that marks the beginning of the year with an entirely different date. In the earliest times the end of the old year and beginning of the new one was always a time for celebration. The time of the new year varied from one society or religion to another, in midwinter or at planting time, but it always called for much noise. Americans can justifiably feel that they have long been preeminent in the field of exuberant and high-spirited New Year's celebrations.

Old Acquaintances

Until the early years of this century, the genteel practice in this country was for friends and relations to exchange both gifts and visits on New Year's Day.

Another custom that still survives is that of eating some form of pork on the first day of the year. Whether the dish is roast suckling pig or the ham hocks and beans popular in the South, the origin is Middle European. The symbolism is direct: this is the time for looking ahead and a hog, unlike the goose or turkey served a week earlier for Christmas dinner, characteristically roots *forward* when foraging for food. Also, in a time before diets and food warnings, fat was good. Serving pork was a symbolic supplication for a fat year—a prosperous future.

The Christmas Coach (1935)

Boy and Cupid (1924)

Valentine's Day

Saint Valentine's Day, February 14, is the day we make an outward show of affection to people we hold dear. Though named for a saint—there is no way of telling which of the three Saint Valentines, all born on February 14, is *the* Saint Valentine—it has no discernable religious significance, and apparently never did.

Nevertheless, Valentine's Day has been celebrated since the Middle Ages. In former times, it was believed the birds mated on February 14 in honor of one Saint Valentine or another.

Tokens of Affection

Of course, the Victorians, on both sides of the Atlantic, developed the lacy Valentine cards and flowery sentiments that set the pattern for the modern Valentine observance. For longer than anyone can say, Valentine's Day has been for lovers.

In the matter of love, Americans of the first half of the twentieth century were considerably more reticent than in the current age, and Norman Rockwell's Valentine's Day paintings reflect this. They are about sentimentalizing, flirtation, and romancing. In the days of the Twenties and early Thirties—people did not flaunt passion or advertise deep commitment. They did, however, freely announce in the words of a popular song, "Yes sir, that's my baby."

Willie Was Different (1967)

Arbor Day

Arbor Day may very well be a holiday whose time has come, in view of the conservation and preservation of the environment. It had a homespun start in 1872, when a man named J. Sterling Morton succeeded in having it established in Nebraska, to stem the soil erosion he had observed there. His obvious solution, then as now, was to plant trees.

Traditionally, the president plants a tree on the White House grounds each April 27, and Arbor Day is observed as a tree-planting day in every state but Alaska. Arbor Day is observed on the third Friday in January in Florida; April 22 in Nebraska; the last Friday in April in Utah; and whatever date the governor selects in Wyoming. In West Virginia, there are two Arbor Days each year: one in the spring and one in the fall.

A Living Legend

It is an appropriate time to recall John Chapman, who in his own lifetime became a legend along the Western frontier as "Johnny Appleseed." Chapman spent most of his life as a missionary and traveler, and always carried a gunny-sack filled with apple seeds, with which he planted countless orchards. He died in 1845, in Indiana. Many an apple tree survived him, and his legend and spirit are still alive.

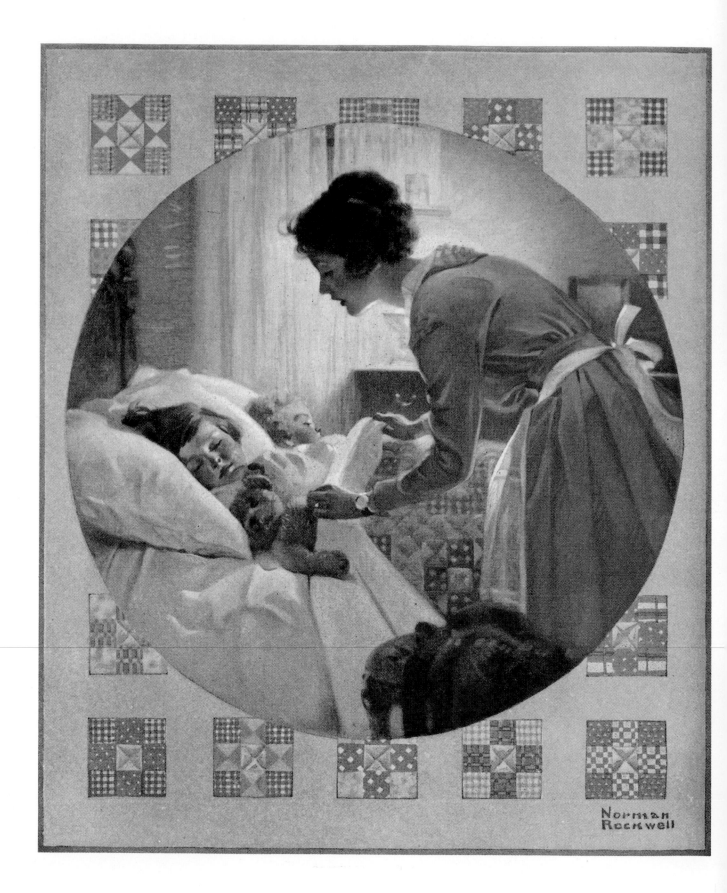

Mother Tucking Children into Bed (1921)

Mother's Day

The first Mother's Day observance in the United States was on May 10, 1908, in the Andrews Methodist Church, in Grafton, West Virginia. The observance came after a patient campaign by Anna M. Jarvis, a spinster who taught Sunday School in the church for 20 years. Miss Jarvis was devoted to her mother, Anna Reese Jarvis, who had died in 1905. After that first service, a tribute to Mrs. Jarvis rather than all mothers, Miss Jarvis expanded her vision.

By 1910, the governor of West Virginia proclaimed a statewide Mother's Day, as did the governors of Oklahoma and Washington. By 1911, Mother's Day was observed in every state, in China, Japan, several African countries, Mexico and Canada. For years, Miss Jarvis traveled the country to promote her tribute to motherhood. But she came to regret the energy and devotion she had put into Mother's Day. She deplored the cards and gifts, the sales and advertisements, and ostentatious displays of later Mother's Days, and dismissed them as commercialization. She had become blind, and was both needy and disillusioned when she died in 1948.

The idea for which she worked so earnestly survives her. Mother's Day, the second Sunday in May, remains universally popular.

Father's Day

By coincidence, the first American Father's Day was also observed in West Virginia, and was the brain-child of a devoted daughter as well. Mrs. John Bruce Dodd, of Spokane, Washington first urged fellow-Americans to honor fathers. She was devoted to her widowed father, William Jackson Smart, who raised her and her five brothers.

In 1916, President Woodrow Wilson proclaimed a national Father's Day, as did Calvin Coolidge, in 1924. Senator Margaret Chase Smith, of Maine, introduced a resolution to establish a permanent national Father's Day in 1957, but it was 1972 before President Richard M. Nixon signed a joint resolution passed by Congress establishing Father's Day, but omitting any recurring date. Father's Day is customarily observed on the third Sunday in June.

There is an ancient precedent for Father's Day. In Rome, Parentalia, from February 13 to 22, was the time of homage to departed parents.

Dinner Jacket (1963)

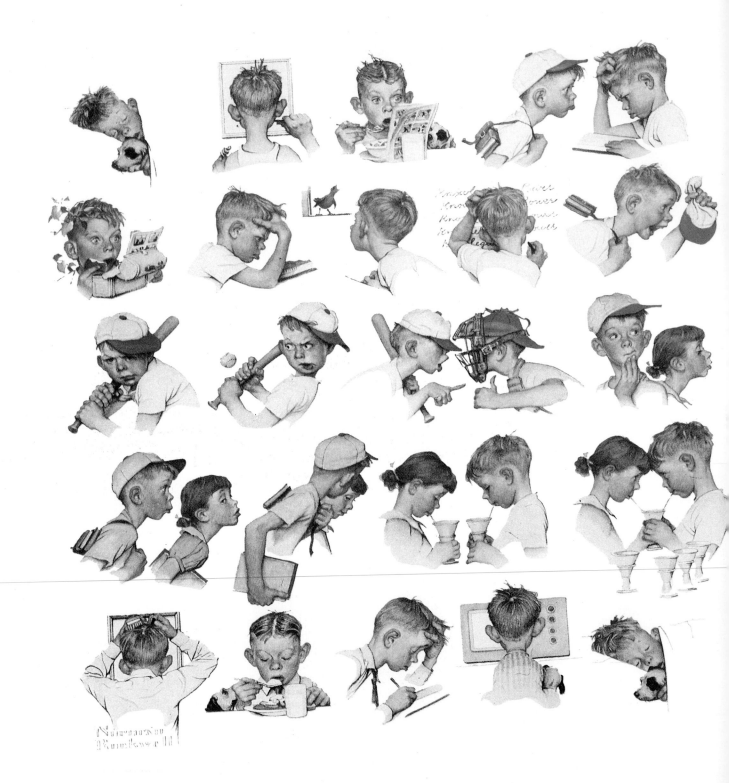

Day in the Life of a Little Boy (1952

Chapter III

Holidays for Children

Children participate in holidays with body and soul—totally invigorated. Their exuberance shines through Norman Rockwell's art. Several holidays seem tailored for children to exercise their ingenuity and express their special talents.

April Fool Fishing (1945)

April Fool's Day

No one seems to know the origins of April Fool's Day, but it is dear to the hearts of American school children. It is recorded as far back as the Eighteenth Century in Britain and France, where it was observed by sending gullible people on pointless errands and by playing practical jokes in much the same fashion as it is marked in this country today.

Easter (1955)

84

Easter

Easter, in the Western church calendar, falls on the first Sunday following the full spring moon, and its observance incorporates the symbols, such as eggs and chicks and the rabbits and hares, that characterized pre-Christian spring fertility festivals.

New Beginnings

It is the season of flowers, and the season of new beginnings. Since it can occur in either early or late spring, Easter heralds the earliest flowers and the urge to begin the garden. New clothes and new hats are a prerequisite for the Easter parade. A choir boy makes a last-minute effort to slick down his cow-lick. Females throughout the land primp before mirrors in their Easter finery.

Planting the Garden (1962)

From Time Immemorial

In earliest Rome, eggs were given as prizes to winners of Easter foot-races run on oval race-courses. The ancients took their symbols seriously, and literally. It was the hare that represented the spring, or planting moon, because hares are born with their eyes open and rabbits are not. Another precursor of the Easter Bunny was the hare-like egg symbol of the Anglo-Saxon goddess of spring, Eostre. The Japanese have a high regard for the spring hare.

Stained Glass Window (1960)

Easter Finery

Many Easter symbols and customs are direct and unequivocal. The Easter Parade is a direct descendent from the Emperor Constantine who required his council to wear finery to celebrate the resurrection. The custom of buying new bonnets and other apparel for the day is rooted in the ages-old superstition that new clothes at Easter bring luck for the year. The custom of rolling eggs on the White House lawn and other lawns is an ancient one, symbolic of rolling the stone away from the sepulcher.

Girl Choosing Hat (1931) 91

Culinary Customs

Hot cross buns on Good Friday are an adaptation from ancient rites, in which many peoples and tribes baked pastries as offerings. The Anglo-Saxons baked buns for their spring festival, and early missionaries added the cross of icing as a blessing. On one Good Friday in the eighteenth century, it was reported that 50,000 Londoners besieged the Old Chelsea Bun House and bought 150,000 hot cross buns. Another culinary custom, eating pancakes on Shrove Tuesday, is believed to be grounded on the need to use the flour, fat, and sugar that would not be needed for the 40-day Lenten fast.

Rural Vacation (1938)

Springtime: Boy with Rabbit (1935)

May Day

May Day, the spring festival, has celebrated the first spring planting, the renewal of life, since time immemorial. It is quite recognizable as the feast day for Flora, the Roman goddess of flowers. It was the beginning of the year for the Druids, a time for purification. In Sweden, May Day was at one time the occasion for mock battles between men representing winter and summer.

Traditions

Earlier in this century in America, May Day was observed in schools and on playgrounds. Children prepared May baskets with strips of colored paper and strung together flowers for decorations. They danced around the maypole, plaiting and unplaiting gaily colored strips of cloth or paper, fastened to the top of the pole.

The tradition is still celebrated in Britain, especially in rural villages, where the May pole is decorated and both children and adults celebrate with dancing. It could be that all that scrambling was the source for the World War II aviators' radio distress call, "Mayday! Mayday!"

Barefoot Boy Playing Flute (1938) 97

A Celebration of Spring

In earlier times, both in Britain and the United States, it was the custom to "bring in the May." People gathered flowers and branches to decorate their homes. The community selected a local girl as the Queen of May, and on May Day the young men drew her through the town on a cart.

May heralds the spring flowers, the renewal of foliage in which rabbits and other browsers can safely forage for succulent new shoots. It also used to be the time for the dreaded spring tonic, usually composed of sulphur and molasses.

The Music Master (1920)

Prom Time

Spring is the time for romance and for school proms. Sweethearts are resplendent in their formal prom dress, and starry-eyed with thoughts of their futures, together or apart. For each heart that may have been broken on prom night, there was another that had pledged eternal love.

Prom Dress (1949)

Grandfather Frightened by Jack-o-Lantern (1920)

Halloween

Halloween embodies spirits of imps and hobgoblins, who lived in ancient times and in the minds of little children. Named after All Hallows' Eve, Halloween is a special holiday which gives children the chance to dress up in costume and visit their elders with that infamous demand for sweets, "Trick or Treat."

By the end of October, people are ready for a holiday. The promise of autumn and Indian summer starting with Labor Day weekends has been fulfilled. The harvest festivals are to come with Thanksgiving. And, as with most American holidays, there is ample historical precedent for a holiday on October 31. The Celtic Druids in Wales, Ireland, the Scottish highlands, and Brittany, celebrated New Year's Day November 1.

The Jack-o-Lantern

The Jack-o-Lantern has an Irish story behind it. The legend is that Jack, a renowned drinker and mischief-maker, once tricked the devil into climbing a tree to get some juicy apples. He quickly carved the sign of the cross on the tree trunk, marooning Satan himself in the upper branches. Jack made the devil swear never to come after his soul again if he let him down, and the deal was struck. When Jack died and presented himself at the pearly gates, St. Peter sent him to the devil anyway. But the devil, still smarting from that apple tree trick, rejected Jack. He threw a coal from the fires of hell at Jack, who has been wandering between heaven and hell ever since.

Man Playing Violin (1921)

Trick or Treat

In Colonial times, October 31 was called "Mischief Night" and "Nutcrack Night." Until well into the twentieth century, the treats distributed to diminutive ghosts and goblins were mainly apples and nuts. These same gifts were distributed in ancient Rome. The mischief, which by the early twentieth century had become the tricks, were fairly harmless stuff: ringing doorbells and running away; taking gates off their hinges; overturning outhouses.

If the tricks have undergone some changes—after all, how often in modern America do you find an outhouse to overturn?—the old elements of witch and goblin costumes and children trooping from door to door survive.

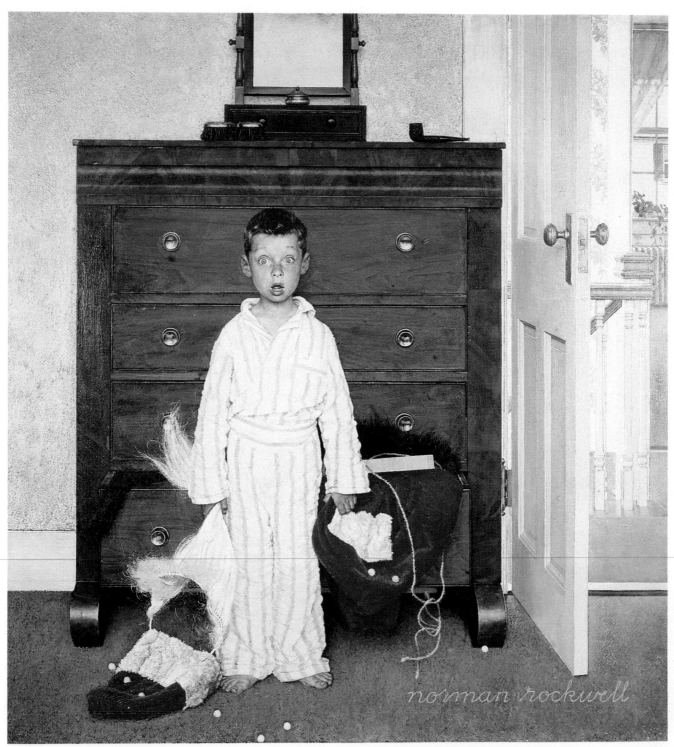

The Discovery (1956)

Chapter IV

Family Holidays

Thanksgiving and Christmas seem to be the favorite holidays of the year and Norman Rockwell recorded them with extraordinary insight. It is the one season for homecoming, for the gathering of families. Perhaps this, combined with the nostalgia Americans have always felt for the good old days, accounts for the popularity of these two holidays.

Thanksgiving

Thanksgiving starts with the Pilgrims, those hardy and dour souls who arrived at Plymouth Rock, Massachusetts, in November, 1620, and celebrated their harvest and their survival in the wilderness the following year.

Neither turkey nor pumpkin pie were part of the first Thanksgiving menu. The wild turkeys the Pilgrims encountered were extremely wily and elusive birds, not at all like our unintelligent domestic variety. The barnyard turkey did not then exist. It is a source of confusion that the guinea fowl brought over on the Mayflower were called turkeys, simply because the first guinea fowl seen in England had come from Turkey.

It was a men-only celebration, and it lasted three days. Thirteen women had died in that hard first year, and it was left to four women and two teenage girls to prepare the banquet.

In addition to venison, there was goose and local seafood, as well as eels, white bread, cornbread, leeks, watercress, and a variety of greens. For dessert, there were wild plums and dried berries.

Thanksgiving (1919)

The First Feast

An indian named Squanto joined the Pilgrims and remained with them until his death, in 1622. It is possible that without his help, the colony would not have survived that first winter. Squanto helped the Englishmen build their houses, and he instructed them in the ways of tracking the local game and finding the wild fruits and berries needed to supplement their ship-borne stock of food. Squanto had also instructed his new friends on cultivating the native corn (he specified that a fish be planted in each corn-hill), how to construct fish traps, and how to net herring. Despite the hardships and deaths, the Pilgrims had a lot to be grateful for on that first Thanksgiving. They had shelter—seven houses and seven other buildings. They had harvested 20 acres of corn, but harvested nothing from six acres planted with wheat, barley, and peas.

The bounty of corn even permitted an increase in the ration of corn-meal. It seemed the colony, in spite of everything, was well launched. So the Pilgrims celebrated in style. They invited Massasoit, chief of the Wampanoags, who came with 90 braves. The colonists paraded, discharged blank charges in their muskets, and sounded bugles. They played stool ball, a game that resembled croquet. The colonists and Indians competed in races and jumping games, and the Indians demonstrated their skill with bow and arrow.

The Indians outnumbered the Pilgrims two to one, and they brought five deer to the feast with them.

A Pilgrims Progress (1921)

A Family Affair

Most of Norman Rockwell's Thanksgiving paintings—especially in his early years—refer closely to Thanksgiving traditions. The artist's characteristic light touch and observations of the human condition sparkle in his Thanksgiving art.

He brings to life the joy that families share at this special holiday. Family gatherings, replete with enough food to feed an army, set the tone for the beginning of this special holiday season.

Thanksgiving: Mother and Son Peeling Potatoes (1945)

CHRISTMAS

Gramps in the Snow (1937)

116

Christmas

Christmas is a just about everyone's favorite holiday. While it is a time of Santa and gifts, of wonder and joy to children, it is much more to the grownups. It is the greatest family holiday of all. As far back as we can remember, from the appearance of that first street-corner Santa ringing his brass bell at his station next to the big cast-iron pot, anticipation and tension grew. By December 24, the radio was broadcasting little other than Christmas carols, the children were agog with excitement.

The Anticipation

By the time of Norman Rockwell and his several generations of contemporary Americans, the Christmas celebration had been well established for as far back as most people remembered. Americans embraced all the symbols and customs of Christmas. It is a religious holiday, but Americans, following the British tradition, have always emphasized the merry part of Merry Christmas.

Ours is the old-time English Christmas, with only a few alterations. The domestic turkey, dressing, and cranberry sauce quickly replaced the Christmas goose so beloved by Dickens' characters. Our American contribution, pumpkin pie, doesn't seem to have made any converts overseas.

Children Looking in Toy Store Window (1920)

A Joyous Holiday

It seems we've always exchanged Christmas cards. But the cards, too, are a fairly modern development. They were first exchanged in England in the 1840s and were decorated mostly with floral designs. Religious scenes appear to be a twentieth century development.

Christmas carols and the custom of strolling through the town or neighborhood and singing to the people in their homes, is authentically an English heritage, and an old one.

When Norman Rockwell began his career early in the twentieth century, Americans were celebrating Christmas in much the fashion we do today. We exchanged cards, sang carols, trimmed trees, prepared for the feast. Americans bought and hid Christmas presents and complained about the commercialization of the good old holiday, just as we do now, and counted the shopping days 'til Christmas.

It is all very jolly and very happy, as it always was. And somehow, after all the shopping, wrapping, cooking, traveling, and tensions, we remember what it is about: peace on earth, good will toward men.

Christmas: Santa's Christmas List (1924)

The Day!

Christmas is a religious holiday, to be sure, but it is also very much a secular holiday. It is in this secular sense, as a season to be jolly, that Norman Rockwell portrayed Christmas, just as he did many other holidays. To Americans of all generations, Santa Claus and the spirit of giving were and are the personifications of Christmas. This same spirit of giving need not be limited to one holiday, one time a year. Norman Rockwell knew and painted that very spirit.

Girl with Christmas Doll (1917)

123

Picture Credits: